First printing, 2023.

Roger Schroeder
1127 Quivira Dr.
Colorado Springs, Colorado, 80910

Support@sofakingrad.com

To:_____

From:_____

_____

_____

_____

What do you call someone who points out the obvious?

Someone who points out the obvious.

Why can't you hear a psychiatrist go to the bathroom?

Because the 'P' is silent!

How do lawyers say goodbye?

We'll be suing ya!

What do you call a pig that does karate?

A pork chop.

Why did the scarecrow win an award?

Because he was outstanding in his field.

Did you hear about the guy who invented Lifesavers?

They say he made a mint.

I was thinking about starting a business that sold only puzzles.

But I could never put it all together.

I'm thinking about starting a business that sells only wind chimes.

It's a breeze.

What do you call a group of cows playing instruments?

A moo-sical band.

What did the shoes say to the pants?

SUP, BRITCHES!

What do you call a fake noodle?

An impasta.

I'm reading a book on the history of glue.

I just can't seem to put it down.

When does a joke become a dad joke?

When it becomes apparent!

Did you hear about the Italian chef that died?

He pasta way.

I was wondering why the ball was getting bigger.

Then it hit me.

I'm addicted to brake fluid.

But I can stop anytime.

Where does the king keep his armies?

Up his sleevies

Why should you not write with a dull pencil?

Because it's pointless.

What do you call a snowman with a six-pack?

An abdominal snowman.

Why did the bicycle fall over?

Because it was two-tired.

Did you hear about the restaurant called Karma?

You get what you deserve.

I used to have a job at a calendar factory

But I got fired for taking a couple of days off.

I'm a big fan of whiteboards.

They're re-markable.

I'm reading a book on the history of stairs.

It's a step-by-step guide.

I'm thinking about opening up a store that sells only pencils.

The idea is pointless, but it's worth a shot.

Why do scientists hate atoms?

Because they make up everything.

Why do cows wear bells?

Because their horns don't work.

Why don't seagulls fly by the bay?

Because then they'd be bay-gulls.

What do you call a bear with no teeth?

A gummy bear.

Why is it inappropriate to make a 'dad joke' if you're not a dad.

It's a faux pa.

Why did the blind man fall In the well?

Because he couldn't see that well!

I used to play piano by ear.

Now I use my hands.

Why do chicken coops only have two doors?

Because if they had four, they'd be a chicken sedan.

I was going to make a belt out of watches,

but then I realized it would be a waist of time.

Why did the mushroom go to the party?

Because he was a fungi to be with.

Why did GI in the Army go to the party?

Because he was a fungi to be with.

Why don't they play poker in the jungle?

Too many cheetahs.

Why did the math book look sad?

Because it had too many problems.

I'm thinking about starting a business that sells only calendars.

It's a timely idea.

I'm once had a business that sold only post-it notes.

I got out of it because there were too many sticky situations.

I'm thinking about starting a business that sells only birdhouses.

It's for the birds.

Why did the football coach go to the bank?

To get his quarterback.

Why do birds fly south for the winter?

Because it's too far to walk.

I'm thinking about starting a business that sells only paintbrushes.

It's a stroke of genius.

I'm thinking about becoming a lawyer,

but I'm not sure I have the briefs for it.

Why don't eggs tell jokes?

Because they'd crack each other up.

I'm thinking about starting a business that sells only drumsticks.

It's a sound investment.

Why did the computer go to the doctor?

Because it had a virus.

Why did the bear break up with his girlfriend?

She was too grizzly.

I'm thinking about starting a business at a golf course that sells only doughnuts.

It's a hole in one.

Why did the traffic light turn red?

Because it wanted to stop traffic.

What do you call a pile of cats?

A meowtain.

I'm reading a book on gravity.

It's impossible to put down.

Why don't you ever see elephants hiding in trees?

Because they're so good at it.

Why should you never eat a clock?

It's too time consuming!

Why do pirates have parrots on their shoulders?

Because they can't afford earrings.

Why did the hip guy burn his tongue?

Because he drank his coffee before it was cool.

Why don't ants get sick?

They have anti-bodies.

Why don't skeletons fight each other?

They don't have the guts.

What did the grape say when it got stepped on?

Nothing, it just let out a little whine.

Why do elephants never use computers?

They're afraid of the mouse.

Why did the coffee file a police report?

It got mugged.

I'm trying to organize a hide and seek tournament,

but it's really hard to find good players.

What do you call a can opener that doesn't work?

A can't opener.

Why did the man get hit by a bicycle every day?

He was stuck in a vicious cycle.

Why don't bicycles ever tell jokes?

They're two tired.

I'm thinking about starting a business that sells only stairs.

Many say it's a step in the right direction.

I'm thinking about becoming a fortune teller,

but I don't see a future in it.

I'm reading a book about teleportation.

It's bound to take me somewhere.

Did you hear about the mathematician who's afraid of negative numbers?

He'll stop at nothing to avoid them.

What do you get when you cross a snowman and a shark?

Frostbite.

Why don't oysters give to charity?

Because they're shellfish.

I'm writing a book on the history of glass.

I can see right through it.

Why did the baker go to therapy?

Because he kneaded help.

Why did the cookie go to the doctor?

Because it felt crummy.

I used to be a baker,

but I couldn't make enough dough.

Why did the banana go to the doctor?

Because it wasn't peeling well.

Why did the teddy bear say no to dessert?

Because it was already stuffed.

Why do bees hum?

Because they don't know the words.

Why don't zombies eat clowns?

Because they taste funny.

What do you call an alligator in a vest?

An investi-gator.

I'm thinking about getting a new job as a professional window cleaner.

It's a job I can really see myself doing.

I'm thinking about getting a job at a cheese factory,

but I'm afraid I won't make the cut.

Why did the golfer wear two pairs of pants?

In case he got a hole in one.

I'm thinking about getting a job at the circus,

but I'm afraid I'll just be clowning around.

What did one wall say to the other?

I'll meet you at the corner."

What do you call a man who can't stand?

Neil.

What do you call a cheese that isn't yours?

Nacho cheese.

Why did the chicken go to the séance?

To talk to the other side.

Why do fish live in saltwater?

Because pepper water makes them sneeze.

I'm thinking about becoming a chef,

but I don't think I have the thyme.

I was thinking about becoming a pirate but I decided not to,

because I can never get any booty.

Why did the melon run away and get married?

Because it cantaloupe.

Why do cows have hooves instead of feet?

Because they lactose.

I'm thinking about starting a business that sells doorknobs.

It's a turn-key operation.

Why do ghosts like to ride elevators?

Because it lifts their spirits.

I'm thinking about becoming a comedian,

but I hate it when people laugh at me.

What do you call a man with no arms or legs in the water?

Bob.

What's red and bad for your teeth?

A brick

What do you call a dinosaur with an extensive vocabulary?

A thesaurus.

Why do trees have so many friends?

They branch out.

Why did the grape stop in the middle of the road?

It ran out of juice.

Why did the man put his money in the freezer?

He wanted cold hard cash.

Did you hear about the kidnapping at the park?

She woke up.

What do you call a boomerang that doesn't come back?

A stick.

What did the duck say when it bought lipstick?

"Put it on my bill."

Why are ducks always mad?

Because they have bills.

What do you call a chicken that crosses the road, rolls in the dirt, and comes back?

A dirty double-crossing chicken.

Why did the man stare at a can of orange juice for hours?

Because it said concentrate.

Why do scuba divers fall backwards off the boat?

Because if they fell forward they'd still be in the boat.

Why did the farmer name his pig "Ink"?

Because it kept running out of the pen.

What do you call a pony with a cough?

A little hoarse.

What do gay horsies eat?

Hay

What do you call a snobbish criminal going down stairs?

A condescending con descending.

What do you call a bee that can't make up its mind?

A maybe.

Why can't you give Elsa a balloon?

Because she'll let it go.

Why was the computer cold?

It left its Windows open.

What do you call a lazy kangaroo?

A pouch potato.

I'm reading a book about teleportation.

It's bound to take me places.

How many tickles does it take to make an octopus laugh?

Ten-tickles.

I don't trust people who do acupuncture.

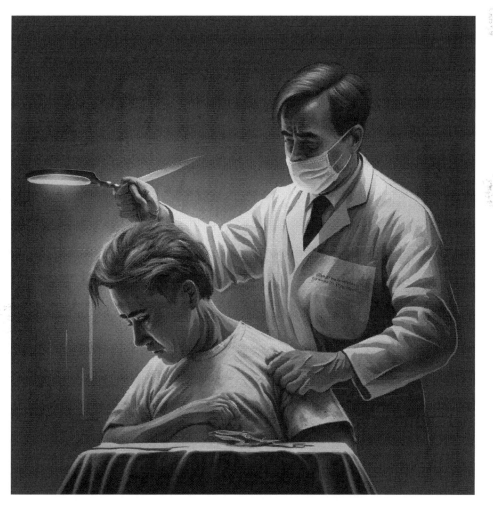

They're back stabbers.

What did the janitor say when he jumped out of the closet?

"Supplies!"

What do you call a person with a rubber toe?

Roberto.

What do you call a sleeping bull?

A bulldozer.

Why do ducks make great detectives?

They always quack the case.

Why did the fireman wear red suspenders?

To keep his pants up.

Why do melons have weddings?

Because they cantaloupe.

What do you call a snake who works for the government?

A civil serpent.

Why did the teddy bear say no to dessert?

Because it was already stuffed.

Why did the bird join the military?

He wanted to be a paratrooper.

What did the hat say to the scarf?

You hang around while I go on ahead.

Why did the tree go to the dentist?

To get a root canal.

Why do bees have sticky hair?

Because they use honeycombs.

Why wont cats go to the beach at Christmas?

They don't like sandy claws.

I told my wife she was drawing her eyebrows too high.

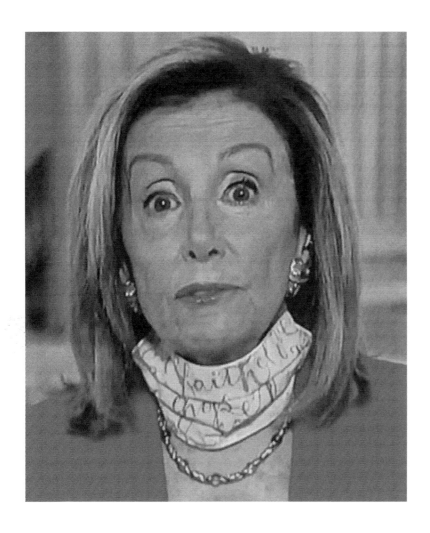

She looked surprised.

Why did the grape stop in the middle of the road?

Because it ran out of juice.

Why don't bicycles ever tell jokes?

Because they are wheely tire-rd.

Why did the duck cross the road?

To prove he wasn't a chicken.

What do you call a fish wearing a bowtie?

Sofishticated.

What did the sushi say to the bee?

Wasabi!

Why did the grapefruit go out with the prune?

Because it couldn't get a date.

Why did the chef get arrested?

He was caught beating the eggs.

Why did the turkey refuse dessert?

Because it was already stuffed.

Why don't skeletons like parties?

*They have **no body** to dance with.*

What do you call a camel with three humps?

Pregnant.

What did the daddy spider say to the baby spider?

"You spend too much time on the web."

What do you get when you cross a sheep and a kangaroo?

A woolly jumper.

What do you call a fly without wings?

A walk.

What do you get when you cross a horse with a unicorn?

A uni-horned horse.

Why don't pandas like to go to school?

They don't like being bamboo-zled.

Why did the turtle cross the road?

To get to the shell station.

What do you call a bear with no socks on?

Barefoot.

Why did the monkey fall out of the tree?

Because it was dead.

Why did the chef add sugar to his soup?

He wanted to sweeten the pot.

What do you call a rabbit with fleas?

Bugs Bunny.

Why did the kangaroo stop drinking coffee?

Because it made him jumpy.

Why did the snake go to the doctor?

It had a hisstory of shedding.

What do you call a group of frogs that love hip-hop?

Rap-tiles.

What did the baker say to the pie?

You're a little crusty.

Why did the baker refuse to make any bread today?

She kneaded a break.

How did the baker get rich?

His business was on the rise.

What do you call the school chef who worked her way up to become a principal?

A stew-perintendent.

What do you get when you cross a horse, a donkey and a bartender?

A honkey-tonk.

Why don't ducks tell jokes?

Because they don't want to quack each other up.

Why did the octopus beat the shark in a fight?

Because it was well-armed.

What do you call a bear with no ears?

B.

Why don't dinosaurs drive cars?

Because they're extinct.

Why did the student take a ladder to school?

To get to high school.

Why did the music teacher go up to the roof?

To reach the high notes.

Why did the student bring a hammer to school?

To nail his test.

Why don't dogs dance?

Because they have two left feet.

What do you get when you cross a pig and a centipede?

Bacon and legs.

Why don't sharks like fast food?

They can't catch it.

Why don't bears wear shoes?

They prefer bear feet.

What do you call a happy kangaroo?

A hop-timist.

Why did the sad kangaroo break up with her boyfriend?

He was too hoppy.

Why did the duck go to the doctor?

It was feeling a little down.

Why did the owl invite his friends over?

To have a hootenanny.

Why did the student bring a calculator to school?

To multiply his chances of success.

I burnt my Hawaiian pizza today.

I should have put it on aloha temperature.

What did the baker say to the bread?

You knead me.

Why don't sharks play basketball?

They're afraid of the net.

What do you get from a pampered cow?

Spoiled milk.

What do you get when you cross a snake and a pie?

A python.

Why do horses have passports?

So they can travel any neigh-where.

What do you get when you cross a sheep and a porcupine?

An animal that knits its own sweaters.

Why did the cat sit on the computer?

To keep an eye on the mouse.

Why did the kangaroo stop drinking coffee?

Because it made him jumpy.

Why did the teacher wear sunglasses to class?

Because her students were so bright.

Why did the zebra go to jail?

It was wearing stripes.

Why did the student eat his homework?

Because his teacher told him it was a piece of cake.

Why did the computer go to school?

To get smarter.

Why did the teacher write on the window?

Because she wanted her lesson to be crystal clear.

What did the duck say to the bartender?

"Put it on my bill."

What did the carrot say to the tomato?

Lettuce be friends.

What do you call a snake that works for a bakery?

A pie-thon.

What did the butcher say when he backed into the meat grinder?

Looks like I'm behind on my work.

Did you hear about the two potatoes that had a cooking competition?

They had a fry-off.

Why did the grape go out with the raisin?

Because it was a date.

A jumper cable walks into a bar and the bartender says,

your not going to try to start anything are you?

Why can't a nose be 12 inches long?

Because then it'd be a foot!

What did one twin say to the other?

There's not enough womb in here for the two of us!

What did the finger say to the thumb?

I'm in glove with you.

Our wedding was so beautiful...

even the cake was in tiers!

Why does a tuna age about five times faster than a human?

Because tuna half-hours are equal to 150 minutes!

Why did the picture go to jail?

Because he was framed!

A Mexican magician tells the audience he will disappear on the count of 3.

*He says, "Uno, dos..." and then *poof* ... he disappeared without a tres!*

What was the foots favourite type of chips?

Dori-toes!

What does a clock do when it's hungry?

It goes back four seconds!

What do sprinters eat before a race?

Nothing, they fast.

Why cant zoo animals take tests?

There are too many cheetahs!

Did you hear about the restaurant on the moon?

They serve great food, but there's no atmosphere!

I broke my arm in two places, and do you know what my doctor told me?

You really gotta to stay out of those places!

Who invented the round table?
Sir Cumference!

People tell me that I am ignorant and Apathetic.

I tell them I don't know and I don't care what they think

Two cows are talking in a field. One cow says "MOOOOO!"

The other cow said pretty much the same thing.

Why don't blind people go skydiving?

Because it scares their dogs too much.

What is invisible and smells like carrots?

Rabbit farts

What did one elevator say to another elevator?

I think I'm coming down with something!

Why was the snowman looking through a bag of carrots?

He was picking his nose!

What did one snowman say to the other snowman?

It smells like carrots out here!

What did the green grape say to the purple grape?

Breathe dammit, BREATHE!

What do you get when you divide the circumference of a Jack-o-lantern by its diameter?

Pumpkin Pi!

What role do green beans play in Thanksgiving dinner?

The casse-role!

What sound does a nut make when it sneezes?

Cashew!

What did the mother Buffalo say when her boy left for college?

Bye Son!

Did you hear about the two satellites that decided to get married?

The wedding wasn't much, but the reception was incredible!

Why did the tomato turn red?

Because it saw the salad dressing!

What did the Mexican firefighter name his two sons?

José and Hose B.

How many apples grow on a tree?

All of them!

What do you call an empty jar of cheese whiz?

Cheese Was!

Why did the cookie cry?

Because his mother was a wafer so long!

How much does a skeleton weigh?

A skeleTON!

What did the policeman say to his belly button?

You're under a vest!

Did you hear about the circus fire?

It was intense!

Why are ghosts banned from the liquor store?

Because they would steal all the boos!

What did Snow White say when she came out of the photobooth?

Someday my prints will come...

Did you hear the one about the magic tractor?

It was driving down the road when it suddenly turned into a field!

What is the number one cause of divorce?

Marriage!

What's a ghoul's favorite bean?

A human bean!

How many lives does a Nazi cat have?

Nien!

What did the teacher do with the student's cheese report?

She "grated" it!

What do hillbillies drink out of?

Hiccups!

What do you give a sick bird?

Tweetment.

Why did the toilet paper roll down the hill?

To get to the bottom.

What did one toilet say to the other toilet?

You look flushed.

What's the best way to carve wood?

Whittle by whittle!

What do you call a large animal from Africa that lets its hair grow?

A hippy-potamus!

What type of shots do computers do?

Screen Shots.

I'm thinking about starting a business that sells only doorknobs made of ice.

It's a cool idea.

What did the red light say to the green light?

Don't look, I'm changing!

I'd like to give a big shout out to all the sidewalks...

for keeping me off the streets!

My dog used to chase people on a bike.

It got so bad, I had to take his bike away!

Why do vampires believe everything you tell them?

Because they're suckers!

Does anyone need an ark?

I Noah guy.

What's large, grey, and doesn't matter?

An irrelephant.

What did the mom say to her son before he got in the car?

"Get in the car."

Why do gorillas have big nostrils?

Because gorillas have big fingers.

Why don't mummies take time off?

They're afraid to unwind!

I sold my vacuum the other day...

all it was doing was collecting dust!

What's the difference between a well dressed man on a unicycle and a poorly dressed man on a bike?

Attire!

A man opens his door and finds a snail on his front porch. He picks it up and throws it across the street.

A year later the man opens his door and finds the same snail on his front porch. The snail looks up and says, "What the heck was that all about!?"

Where do cows go for a first date?

To the moooovies!

Why did Mozart hate chickens?

Because when he asked them who the best composer was, they'd all say "Bach Bach Bach!"

What do you call twins who live together?

Womb-mates!

How do snails fight?

They slug it out!

What's Forrest Gump's email password?

1forrest1

What's the best time to go to the dentist?

Tooth Hurty!

Why are there fences around a graveyard?

Because people are dying to get in!

What do you call a guy who never farts in public?

A Private Tutor!

What did Jay-Z call his girlfriend before they were married?

Feyoncé!

There are 3 types of people in this world...

Those that are good at Math and those that are not.

What kind of car does an egg drive?

A Yolkswagen!

I'm reading a book about anti-gravity.

It's impossible to put down!

What's the difference between the Starship Enterprise and toilet paper?

Nothing, they both orbit Uranus wiping out Klingons!

When is a pool safe for diving?

It deep ends!

Where do skunks go to pray?

To the pew!

Who's the king of the classroom?

The Ruler!

What's brown and rhymes with snoop?

Dr. Dre

What does Miley Cyrus eat on Thanksgiving?

Twerkey!

What's at the bottom of the ocean and shivers?

A nervous wreck.

What did the hard working gardener do when spring arrived?

He wet his plants!

What do you call a blind dinosaur?

Doyouthinkhesaurus

Why was the broom late for the meeting?

It overswept!

Why did Chewbacca crash the Millennium Falcon the first time he flew it?

It was a Wookiee mistake!

Where do Volkswagens go when they get old?

The Old Volks home!

Wanna hear a joke about paper?

Never mind— it's tearable!

What kind of pictures do turtles take?

Shellfies!

Why do dogs float?

Because they're good buoys!

What did the doe say coming out of the woods?

Boy, I'll never do that again for two bucks!

What's the award for being the best dentist?

A little plaque!

What do clouds wear under their shorts?

Thunderpants

How do crazy people get through a forest?

They take the psycho-path!

What did Kim Jong Un say when his father died?

His korea is over!

Made in the USA
Middletown, DE
07 August 2023

36305968R00097